# Andalusia

## Impressions & Reflections

**A travel report by**

**Chris Marfield**

## Book

Andalusia, this beautiful part of Spain, evokes thoughts of wonderful and pleasurable things. Proud flamenco, mighty cathedrals, breathtaking landscapes and a climate that we in Germany can only dream of.

This travelogue describes a round trip in Andalusia and describes the impressions and reflections characterised by the experiences and encounters on this journey.

## Author

Chris Marfield was born and grew up in Hannover, Germany in 1970. Now he lives and works in Berlin.

Chris Marfield

# Andalusia
## Impressions & Reflections

Bibliographic information of the German National Library:

The German National Library lists this publication in the German National Bibliography; detailed bibliographic data is available on the Internet at http://dnb.dnb.de.

© 2020 Chris Marfield

1st edition

E-Mail: chris.marfield@gmail.com

Production and publisher: BoD - Books on Demand, Norderstedt

ISBN: 978-3-7578-9016-2

# Table of Contents

# Preface

Everyone goes through situations in their lives that lead to upheaval. Sometimes this upheaval leads to something good, sometimes to something bad. It is something new and uncertain that makes one doubt, because it is not known what is waiting in the fog ahead.

In the midst of such upheaval, I decided to make an individual journey to Andalusia. This book contains descriptions of my thoughts and impressions during my journey around this wonderful part of Spain.

# Getting started

I sat in the area of the Check Inn and looked out at the big windows of the building, where the rain pattered against the glass and ran down in rivulets. I'd been dreaming about this trip for a long time, until I got to the point where I wondered why I shouldn't just fly. So a fortnight ago I went on the internet and looked for flights. I compared the offers on popular flight search engines like Kayak, Skyscanner and a few others. When I saw a flight for less than 200 euros, I could hardly believe it and booked it without giving it a second thought. A rental car was quickly found through an automobile club and I had a free choice of hotel. November is not the time when Spain is overcrowded, so I was almost certain to find cheap hotels.

I have been to Spain many times, but only as a package holiday tourist to the well-known destinations such as the Balearic Islands, the Canary Islands or the Costa Brava. But I have never travelled this country on my own.

Over the last two weeks I had mentally replayed the journey several times, wondering if I would find the spirituality that had remained hidden from me at home. Now, as I sat here looking up at the grey sky and the pattering rain, spirituality was still a long way off.

A young woman sat two rows in front of me and was watching me. She had full lips and a slightly plump figure. I guessed she was Swiss, which was obvious as the flight to Málaga was via Zurich. She was sitting alone, with only a small travelling bag on her lap. In the same row sat a family with a small child, in a relaxed holiday mood.

Boarding was imminent and the Swiss woman went to the toilet, the man in the family did the same. When she returned, she sat down two seats away from the child, the man returned and inevitably sat down next to her, much to the embarrassment of the sympathetic Swiss woman.

When I boarded the plane, I quickly found my seat. Many seats remained unoccupied, including the two next to me. I took advantage of the rare freedom and spread myself out generously, as decency would otherwise forbid when someone is sitting next to you.

I picked up a stock market magazine I had bought at the airport, leafed through it for a while and made investment plans. It was these little habits and rituals that I liked to escape into in order to feel a little more secure in new situations.

As the plane broke through the clouds, a bright light shone warmly in my face. I looked out of the window and watched the rising November sun. It pierced through the clouds, slowly turning the sky from a dull grey to a bright, shining blue. I fell asleep to the monotonous hum of the engines and the relaxation that had set in.

The stopover in Zurich went smoothly and without any delays. When I landed in Malaga, the first thing I did was pick up the rental car at the airport. I booked an upgrade with the insurance company because the standard fully comprehensive insurance did not cover tyre damage or stone chipping.
The vehicle handover went quickly and before I knew it I was driving towards Marbella in my little Opel Corsa. It was a hectic time on the motorway, with cars driving impatiently and honking their horns in high spirits. I tried to orientate myself, annoying many a driver who was trying to get home quickly in the rush hour.

*View from the plane*

The further I drove from the airport, the more relaxed I felt. Now was the time to take a deep breath
and enjoy the sun, which I drove towards in a good
mood.

# Marbella

The hotel, with one fairly functional room, was located near the beach promenade. It dated from the 1970s, when tourism was booming and buildings of this kind were being erected at lightning speed. It was a plain concrete box, nestled between the other bed castles built above the seafront promenade.

From the balcony I could see the sea. Palm trees lined the beach, and formed a dreamlike panorama with the blue sea, where the last rays of the sun were reflected on the water before being hidden by a few clouds.

After my shopping, which consisted of a piece of cake, two bottles of water and a bottle of San Miguel, I went for a walk along the seafront. The promenade seemed a bit abandoned in the off season. It was slightly cloudy, about 17 degrees. There were very few people around.

In contrast to the high season, when crowds of people bustled about in the bright sunshine, the town now seemed to be in deep hibernation.

I looked around and noticed the contrasts around me. On one side, a beautiful beach and a wonderful view of the vast sea; on the other, the hotel castles you find in many holiday resorts in Spain.

*View from the balcony*

I left the promenade behind me and walked through a park that led me through the bed castles towards the old town. At first glance, the park was nondescript and seemed to be crushed by the surrounding concrete. Then I blocked out the surroundings and looked around.

To my surprise, the park had a certain charm that made it a sight worth seeing. Palm trees were lined up like an avenue, surrounded by neatly trimmed hedges, and in the middle were bronze statues by

Salvador Dalí. As I looked at the sculptures, I had a similar feeling to when I looked at his paintings.

At first I thought I understood what he was trying to say, then I wasn't sure and interpreted his art as I saw it. I don't know if I actually interpreted what he wanted to say ... maybe he just wanted to inspire people to think for themselves. In any case, he achieved one thing. I was inspired by the sculptures.

*Dalí sculptures*

Continuing into the old town, the streetscape changed. Wide streets became narrow alleyways, oppressive concrete buildings became houses with curved metal balcony railings and street lighting that wouldn't have surprised me if candles were lit at night. I could feel the history here and was captivated from the first moment. I strolled along the cobbled streets, past the restaurants and tapas bars and looked at the houses decorated with flowers. Most of the buildings looked very old, but were so well kept that they could have been built just a day ago. It was like stepping back in time as I walked through the alleyways with their lovingly designed gardens and manicured greenery.

Satisfied with this first impression, I returned to the hotel to eat the cake I had bought earlier, which I washed down with some water. I reviewed my initial thoughts and had not yet realised that I had arrived. The many impressions of the day made me very tired and as I lay on my bed, looking out at the low sun, I fell asleep.

When I woke up, it was already dark. The sound of the sea echoed through the room, and on the wall was the softly shimmering light of the moon, reflected on the gentle waves of the sea.

After a quick shower, I walked back towards the old town, strolling through a park and was amazed by the many small details that caught my eye. A bench with mosaics looked oriental, next to it a bench made of decorated metal. They were completely different styles, but they looked so harmonious together in this square, as if they belonged together.

*Park*

On the edge of the old town, I passed an old castle dating back to the time of the Moors. A wall surrounded a large part of the area, preserving thousands of years of history and characterising the image of this old town.

I wondered what it was like when the Moors ruled here. Were people better off or unhappy? What was it like when the Moors were gone again? I could well imagine that people felt a great sense of freedom when the conquerors were driven out. Perhaps it didn't have the significance for people that I imagined, because they may have had other worries. I probably wasn't even able to really imagine it, because my distant perception was completely different to that of the people at the time.

In the centre of the old town was the church of la Encarnación, in front of which was a square with orange trees. I liked it here, so I settled down in a restaurant. I watched the street, which was deserted, and ordered the recommended dish of the house, which the friendly waiter enthusiastically described to me. After the meal I had two more beers and thought about the next part of the journey.

I wanted to see Gibraltar and then go to Jerez, not sure if I would run out of time. I couldn't imagine that there was much to see in Gibraltar, apart from the view of Morocco.

Back at the hotel, I booked my hotel in Jerez for the next day through HRS and then drank the bottle of San Miguel while looking out at the dark sea, with the moon laughing brightly into it.

I thought of the rain-soaked windows at the airport and it seemed like an eternity ago, but it was only this morning. Now I was feeling a little excited and was looking forward to the next day where the adventure awaited me.

*Church la Encarnación*

# Gibraltar

I impatiently checked out without breakfast. A sense of adventure had spread through me and I felt the thrill of euphoria.

On the way to the car, I walked along the beach promenade, which no longer looked as grey as it had the day before. It was a beautiful sunny day which gave me the feeling that I had finally arrived in Spain.

The journey to Gibraltar turned out to be uncomplicated. While the motorway from the airport to Marbella was full of angry drivers the day before, it was very relaxed from Marbella to Gibraltar. There were only a few cars on the road, so I was able to drive slowly without disturbing anyone and enjoy the scenery.

I had been on the road for less than an hour and Gibraltar was still some 50 kilometres away when I could see the rock in the distance. It towered over the barren landscape and filled me with a mixture of admiration and respect.

Impressed by the beauty of this region, I drove towards the end of Europe in a good mood in the most pleasant Spanish sunshine.

*On the way to Gibraltar*

I quickly found a car park on the Spanish side and treated myself to two breakfast burgers and a coffee at McDonalds. I checked my emails and WhatsApp on my phone and then set off on my walk.

Luckily I had my jogging shoes with me, because I spontaneously decided to climb this imposing and likeable rock on foot.

After crossing the border, I stood in front of a red light and was amazed when an airplane took off right in front of me. The way to Gibraltar was along the airport runway and every time a plane took off or landed, the red light came on and people had to wait. It was one of the strangest scenes I have ever experienced and one I will never forget.

*Airport runway*

I then walked through the town towards Upper Rock. Getting away from the crowds of people streaming into the shopping street, I went up the stairs on the left and followed the signs to the track.

When I passed a small shop, I bought two bottles of water. I realised later that it was a good decision as there was no other opportunity.

I struggled up a seemingly endless number of steps. It was good for me, the exertion, the pain in my legs, the fast beating of my heart. It put me in a good mood, even though I was only at the beginning and didn't yet know what was in store for me.

*Track to Upper Rock*

At the foot of the cliff I came across a road that wound its way upwards in serpentines. I followed this road, not knowing how long it would be. It was a steep climb and I had no idea if I would overexert myself on this hike.

Unfortunately, I hadn't done enough research beforehand, which led to this uncertainty. On the other hand, it felt good to be unprepared. I enjoyed the thrill and the burning thighs on the ascent.

Then I reached the first place of interest, an old defensive system. This was not the only place where strong walls and fortifications could be seen, testifying to a determined will to defend.

*defensive system*

As I continued on my way, the road became steeper and steeper. It was harder to breathe and the gradients were extreme in places. I enjoyed the effort immensely, surrounded by this beautiful nature. I stopped at some viewpoints and enjoyed the amazing views over Spain and as far as Morocco on the other side. By this time at the latest, I had taken this place to my heart.

Along with the euphoria about this place, the feeling of adventure was growing. There were signs everywhere warning people not to feed the monkeys, and I wondered if a monkey might jump out of the bushes at any moment.

When I arrived at the cable car station, I made my first longer stop. I strolled along a wall for a while, when suddenly a monkey jumped from a tree directly onto the wall, but took no further notice of me and continued on its way. Then I sighted more monkeys, a whole family of them.

*View of Spain*

I enjoyed the wonderful view of the vast sea glistening in the midday sun. Then I wondered if it wouldn't be better to turn back, as this seemed to be the summit. But I decided to carry on along the path, maybe something else was coming.

In fact, there was still more to go, it wasn't the end yet. More ascents followed, my knee hurt, my calf tweaked, but I felt good. Eventually I reached another summit and climbed up to take a break and enjoy the view.

I didn't want to part with this moment, fascinated by the view of the vast landscape and the mighty rock. I leaned against the railing and looked down. It was hundreds of metres down.

As beautiful as it was up there, I had to get back at some point, so I thought about going back the way I came, but somehow I kept going and my curiosity won out.

So I followed the path and, lo and behold, it still went on. I continued my hike and came to the real last summit of the rock. At this point it would have been time to turn back and enjoy the beautiful views on the way down, but I discovered steps leading down the other side of the rock.

I didn't think twice and descended the stairs. It would have given me no peace not to know what else was there.

*View of the summits*

Some of the steps were quite steep and it was often more like climbing than decent stairs. The descent was close to the rock and the views were breathtakingly beautiful. I was now walking partly on stairs and partly on narrow paths.

Every now and then I came across hikers. They greeted me in a friendly manner and everyone had a smile on their face despite the effort.

A path led me through scree, sometimes through bush, almost like a forest, until I finally reached the Upper Rock viewpoint, which offered the best panoramic views of Africa.

From there I walked down the road towards the town, got lost a few times and arrived back down at the border after a total of five hours.

I was almost a little sad that it was over and wondered if I would find time to come back here again at the end of my tour. I would have loved to experience this place a second time. Here, after a long time, I had managed to think of nothing but the moment, and every moment here was precious.

I drove along the motorway through the dry and beautiful Andalusian desert landscape, which surrounded me like in a Western where the rider trots lonely through the prairie. I almost felt like that lone rider, riding into the sunset through freedom and adventure.

# Jerez

Jerez looked to me like a town out of a traditional Spanish film. Beautiful old houses, orange trees on the pavements and a lot of calmness.

When I checked into the hotel, I realised that English wouldn't get me very far in this part of the country. So I dug up my rudimentary Spanish skills from a dusty corner of my brain and, lo and behold, it worked. I could barely get a coherent sentence out, but the people were so friendly and relaxed that I was able to communicate in the end. At least I understood the receptionist's directions to the hotel's own car park.

Although the hotel was more functional than luxurious, I felt right at home. It was simple, but an original with a charm I couldn't resist.

After resting a bit, I set off in search of a restaurant. Of course I got a bit lost, as I was a reliable constant, but eventually I found what I was looking for. There was a large square in the centre of the town called

Plaza del Arenal. There were beautiful old buildings around the square, palm trees all around and a kind of Christmas pyramid in the middle.

*Plaza del Arenal*

I sat down in a restaurant overlooking the square. It was rustic and simple, with unplastered stone walls and dark wooden tables. A group of men were sitting comfortably at a large table and having a relaxed conversation. From the snippets of words I could make out, I deduced that they were discussing regional politics.

One of the men spoke resignedly about a government decision on the economy that obviously didn't make him happy. Another agreed with him, looking thoughtfully at the glass of red wine in his hand. Some of the men were obviously unemployed, the after-effects of the last crisis from which the country had not really recovered.

After greedily devouring the delicious food, I had another glass of wine and reflected on the exciting day. There were so many impressions that excited me and gave me a feeling of elation. I could feel the physical exertion in my bones, it felt good. The people had won my sympathy with their natural friendliness and composure.

It was late and I had some plans for the next day. So I went back to the hotel and fell into bed exhausted.

I got up early in the morning to explore the town. First I went to the square where I had eaten the day before and started a sightseeing tour without any particular plans.

I walked off and passed the Alcázar, but I didn't go in - I would have been surprised if it had been open so early in the morning.

Then I came to the Cathedral of Jerez, which made an imposing impression on me. The influences of the Orient were clearly recognisable in its construction. The dome reminded me of a mosque, which is what the cathedral used to be.

*Cathedral of Jerez*

For a Monday morning, there were many people walking around the city centre. They didn't necessarily seem purposeful. At home in Germany, people are all purposefully on their way somewhere. People rush to work, to appointments, even to the doctor, as if their lives depended on it. Here everything was relaxed, people strolled leisurely through the streets as if they had all the time in the world.

As I passed an old pub, I realised that it was time for breakfast, so I stopped in. It was a quaint pub, with brick arches as passageways and a long bar with wooden stools in front of it. An elderly man was reading his newspaper and drinking a coffee. I made myself comfortable at a wooden table that stood between two wine barrels.

*Breakfast in the pub*

Then, with my sketchy knowledge of Spanish, I ordered a roll, which was toasted for me, and liver pate, which was served in a large tin with the roll. I had to smile, but I liked the simplicity, just right for this day, this morning. I gratefully savoured my breakfast.

On the way back I passed El Gallo Azul, a round building at the head of a row of baroque-style houses with a clock in front of it that had letters instead of numbers on the dial.

It seemed to be a popular place. Some people were standing and waiting. Two men seemed to have met by chance and were chatting animatedly. Others strolled across the square, oblivious to the surroundings, which they knew only too well and which no longer seemed special to them.

*El Gallo Azul*

# Cádiz

I drove through the dry steppe, desert-like with bright, barren patches that looked as if it hadn't rained for a long time. At the side of the road, clumps of green bushes bravely held out against the dryness. A black metal bull was enthroned on a small hill.

*On the road*

After parking the car in a multistorey car park and saying a hundred prayers that I would find it again, I entered the Plaza de San Juan de Dios, the main square in Cadiz. I looked around and saw half a dozen sights at once, while Segismundo Moret looked down on me proudly.

Even though the temperature had risen to more than 20 degrees Celsius in the meantime, the people were still wearing warm winter clothes.

*Plaza de San Juan de Dios*

I was overwhelmed by the place, not only the town hall square was beautifully decorated. The houses throughout the town were very well preserved, with old black cast iron street lamps and buildings with baroque columns.

I arrived at the cathedral, which gleamed pearly white in the sun. Two towers rose up on the right and left, the front with a concave indentation and beautiful decorations in the middle. I didn't notice a golden dome until I stepped between the towers and it caught my eye, illuminated by the sun.

This building was also impressive from the inside. One of the highlights was a dome resting on pillars in which a statue stood under a crown. In front of it, on either side, were two female figures in golden robes holding crucifixes protectively.

*Cathedral of Cádiz*

I let myself be captured by the magic of this place. It was one of those moments I wanted to hold on to forever. I soaked up all the impressions and took a deep breath to smell the damp, stony odour of the old walls.

I left nothing out, I wanted to see everything, from the ornaments to the paintings and the statues. There was something to discover everywhere in the cathedral. I didn't miss the crypts in the basement, where some of the city's most famous people are buried.

On the way out, I took a few coins and put them in the box of a beggar crouching at the entrance, which he honoured with gratitude.

*Riverside road*

The streets were now full of people, with only a few tourists to be seen. I walked to the sea, where the houses lined up like a film set in the November sun. The cathedral was the centre of everything.

In a shopping district, I spontaneously entered a leather goods shop selling handmade bags, cases and belts. The salesman showed me a wallet and other items on display. He asked me where I was from and what the weather was like in Germany.

A little small talk followed, with friendly words about our respective origins. In the end, I decided on the wallet and was delighted with the handmade bargain and the seller with a good deal.

I took a detour back to the car, enjoyed the flair of this place and let myself be pampered by the mild Spanish sun.

# Arcos

On the way to the white village I stopped at a petrol station. It was lonely in the steppe, nothing around. It was like in an American thriller, when the mass murderer stops at the lonely petrol station and kills the owner for a pack of cigarettes.

As soon as I parked the car at the petrol pump, the petrol attendant came running up and fumbled with the filler cap. When I got out of the car I didn't understand a word he was saying. After a bit of back and forth I realised what he meant and said with a laugh: "Completo".

He had to laugh too and filled the tank.

The white village emerged like an oasis in the Andalusian desert. At the top of a hill rose a castle that stood protectively above the village.

The houses in Arcor were gleaming white, as if the whole village had been blessed, far from any abyss. The streets were empty. The few people I met on the streets were of an age that suggested experience of life.

I was observed silently out of the corner of my eye. People didn't seem to be talking much, just going about their business in silence. Two men were sitting in front of a house playing chess. They looked at the chessboard with stoic composure, without saying a word. One of the men was smoking a pipe, the clouds of smoke spreading across the street like a soft mist.

*The white village*

The tarmac of the street was immaculately smooth. A pavement separating two rows of houses was decorated with red flagstones. The windows of the houses were barred with heavy steel.

I wondered what it would be like to live in this idyll. Everything seemed so peaceful and carefree. But maybe it was just a shell that I perceived, behind which the same abysses were hidden as in so many places in the world.

As I looked through one of the windows, an old woman was looking at me. She was small and had a dark face with deep wrinkles. Her dark eyes were set deep in their sockets. She looked at me motionlessly. I smiled and nodded, and the corners of her mouth moved up a few millimetres. Apart from that, there was no movement in her face, her eyes just looking at me, without me being able to read any mood in them.

I walked between the houses for a while, the sun was almost summery now and my shirt was sticking to my back. Eventually it got too hot for me and I went back to the car, turned on the air conditioning and continued on my way to Seville, which took me off the motorway and along a country road.

# Seville

I woke up in a business hotel just outside the city centre, where I was accommodated at a fair price.

I had decided to explore the city on foot, spontaneously and without any special preparation. After breakfast, I set off for the city centre at around 09:30. It was bitterly cold that morning, something I was not used to. I had three kilometres ahead of me and, as a precaution, I changed sides of the street where the sun was already warming up.

I took a break in a shopping mall to warm up and have a coffee. It was amazing how similar shopping malls were all over the world. The modern mix of bright lights, glass and smooth floors. There were the same displays in the windows, the same brands and the same sales strategies as at home. I wondered where the growth should coming from if all the brands were already selling everything everywhere.

I continued on my way into the city centre, ignoring the signs pointing in a different direction, and to my own astonishment I was right. Despite a few delays in the shopping mall and another department store, I reached the city centre quite quickly.

*On the way in Seville*

As it was still early and not really warm, I decided to go to the Flamenco Museum, which I discovered by chance. I liked flamenco, the fast, rhythmic guitar playing and the powerful, proud dancing. I watched some multimedia demonstrations that showed a lot about the history of flamenco and its influence on the people of Andalusia. Then I looked at the dancers' exhibits and an art gallery in other rooms. The dancers' dresses were skilfully designed, with wide skirts sewn in several layers in folds so that they could fly around better when they swung their hips.

I left the museum and after a few metres I was standing in front of the cathedral. As I entered I marvelled at its enormous size and wondered why I had never heard of this incredible building. I had heard of two or three famous cathedrals, but I had never heard of the masterpieces in Cádiz and Seville.

*Cathedral*

There was a lot to see, some altars with elaborate carvings, decorations and frescoes. There were also beautiful paintings that I looked at for a long time. I was particularly impressed by a painting of an old man crouched on the floor with his hand outstretched in supplication. In the middle of the painting was an angel in a bright light, draped in a red cloth, looking at the man with a gentle gaze.

I spent about ninety minutes there, looking at some things twice just because I liked them. Afterwards I climbed the tower and took some photos of the skyline above the rooftops of Seville.

Not far from the old town was the Plaza de España, a large semicircular square with a canal running through it, which was also semicircular. The sun was shining brightly and I sat down on one of the many stone benches decorated with colourful ceramic patterns.

*Plaza de España*

As I stretched my feet towards a fountain, I observed the people in the square. The average age was much lower than in Arcos or Jerez. They seemed to be students, chilling out and having a good time. Most of them were couples, sitting close together as if they had just fallen in love. A few metres from me, a young man was poking his girlfriend in the side, who screamed and pinched his arm with a laugh whereupon he tickled her.

I looked at my worn-out jogging shoes and realised I wasn't thinking about anything. I used to believe that one always has to think, because somehow it's impossible to do without it. But no, it seemed to work. I was thinking and I wasn't thinking, as if I could control it. I didn't think at all about home, about work, about what I had to do. I didn't even think about the next day or what I wanted to do after this moment. I just sat in the sun and took it all in.

As I sat there quietly, I could feel how much my bones ached. A blister had formed under my left heel, but that didn't bother me. I felt fine.

Through the Parque de María Luisa, which bordered the Spanish Park, I passed the Museum of Popular Art, which was picturesquely reflected in a lake. From there I walked across the park to the Alcázar, where I bought a ticket, even though it was quite late.

The entrance led through a thick wall with two towers, like a castle. Inside, there were open spaces surrounded by ornate walls with filigree decorations and narrow columns. Huge paintings hung in the medieval-style rooms, which were discreetly illuminated.

*Alcázar*

Outside in the garden, several artists were standing in front of their half-finished paintings. One of the painters was wearing a paint-stained shirt that was hanging halfway down his trousers. He was engrossed in his work, painting a tree in front of him with sweeping movements. Under the easel lay a folded painting, carelessly thrown away.

In the low sun, I made my way down to the river. Passing the famous Torre del Oro, an old watchtower that has become a symbol of Seville, I strolled along the river in the warm sunlight.

I sat down on the riverbank, like many people did, and looked at the colourful houses reflected in the water. The sun was slowly setting behind a church spire, the last rays reflecting brilliantly on the surface of the water.

*At the river*

As in the Spanish square before, there were many couples sitting together in the evening sun. I wondered why Paris is called the city of love when there were far more lovers to be seen here.

The sun disappeared and where there had just been a golden yellow sky, it now turned black. Little by little the lights behind the windows came on, forming a sea of lights that continued through the stars in the sky.

I continued on my way towards the city centre, strolling through the shopping district and looked for a restaurant to have dinner. I quickly found what I was looking for and ordered the menu of the day on the waiter's recommendation.

On the way to the taxi afterwards, a Spanish woman came towards me with a proud, upright posture. She looked me in the eye in a way that few people do. I looked away, then back at her, and she continued to look into my eyes, even more intensely. As we passed each other, I turned and saw her turn to give me one last look out of the corner of her eye.

Satisfied, I drove back to the hotel to relax at the end of the evening and book the hotel for the next night.

# Córdoba

Before I travelled on, I had breakfast at the hotel. They had done a good job with the buffet, there was more than enough of everything. There was a good reason why there was so much to choose from. The hotel was hosting a large group of young people who were also expected for breakfast, and the first of them were already milling around the lobby. When the young people came in, I was very relieved at their good behaviour. No noise, no crowds, everyone was calm and relaxed. They had adopted the relaxed attitude of the Andalusians.

The journey continued without any complications. I immediately found the exit towards Córdoba and drove at a crawling pace along the road that wound its way through the steppe like a viper in the desert. It was incredible how beautiful the such a desert can be.

When I arrived in Cordoba, I couldn't find the hotel, or at least I didn't recognise it as mine, and ended up in a car park by chance, where I got my first glimpse of the Mezquita Cathedral. It looked really impressive, so I was already feeling a lot of anticipation. I kept looking for the hotel and when I asked someone, the knot loosened and I realised I was almost there.

I checked in and was delighted to find the first four-star hotel on this trip that at least came close to the stars.

I quickly freshened up and walked to the cathedral. I was again overwhelmed by the size and grandeur of the building, which I entered with appropriate humility. Inside I was also fascinated, although I didn't quite find the spirit of Cádiz or Seville.

The countless red and white striped arches on the pillars, positioned in mathematical regularity through the building, were an eye-catching feature.

Nowhere else have I found the different religions so united as in this cathedral, and that really touched me.

I wondered what it would be like if people of different faiths prayed together here. I liked the idea, even though I would probably not live to see it.

I continued through the old town towards the centre. I walked through the narrow alleyways between the old walls and came out in an unfamiliar square with a monumental building towering in front of me.

*Mezquita in Córdoba*

After a coffee and a piece of cake I had at lunchtime during a stopover, I got lost several times. I learned what it feels like to walk straight ahead with complete conviction and then end up walking in circles.

At some point the coffee started to take effect and I realised there was no toilet to be found anywhere. So I trudged back to the hotel at a fast pace, where I got ready for the evening. I could feel the effects of walking in my body. With new shoes, the blister didn't hurt as much, but everything else did. My body felt pretty sore, but I couldn't get enough and wanted to explore everything.

Now it was time to visit the Alcázar, which I had already heard a lot about. It was a building with old walls that contained a lot of history. I had a great view of the city from the tower and it was also a great place to take photos of the Roman bridge. Some parts of the building were dilapidated and looked like ruins, but I was still interested in them because of their history.

Afterwards I walked through the gardens, which were very nicely designed, with artificial water points and lots of well-tended greenery.

*Roman bridge*

From there I ended up in the Jewish quarter, where I completely lost my bearings once again. I finally found a restaurant to give my tired bones a rest. I had a salad, a potato omelette and a pot of fried chicken.

*Jewish quarter*

It was already dark when I left the restaurant. I walked through the narrow cobbled streets to the Roman bridge, which, like the buildings around it, was bathed in a warm yellow light.

I then made my way back to the hotel to stretch my legs.

*Old Town*

# Granada

On the way to Granada, the motorway wound its way through the mountains. The desert landscape alternated with mountain massifs and the gradients demanded a lot from the car. Just before Granada, large snow-capped mountains appeared behind the city. The contrast was so strong that for a moment I doubted I was still in Spain.

The town looked old and worn, as if nothing had been done for a long time. A dual carriageway ran through the middle of the main road, forcing me to make some daring lane changes. Eventually I found the hotel without any significant detours.

After checking in, I made my way to the Alhambra. The area I walked through looked like a ghetto, but the whole city seemed to be poor. Nowhere else in Spain had I seen so many beggars as here.

The Alhambra was located on a mountain, which had some inclines, but they were harmless compared to Gibraltar. The history of the princely palace was very interesting and Islam was omnipresent. Many buildings were in ruins and there were many beautiful gardens which were lovingly maintained. From the top of the Alhambra I could see the whole city. I loved the view over the city with the mountains behind it. Unfortunately the weather was getting a bit uncomfortable, the clouds were getting thicker and thicker.

*View of the city from the Alhambra*

I took the tour with an electronic audio guide, which flooded me with so much information that I could only memorise a fraction of it.

The Palacios Nazaríes were something like the heart of the complex and the place where the rulers used to stay. The floor and the columns were made of white marble, which was so noble that I couldn't imagine anything else but great rulers living there.

*Lion Court*

Then I passed El Partal, which was beautifully reflected in the smooth water. I walked from one highlight to the next and was overwhelmed by the beauty that surrounded me.

Finally, I walked to the gardens and through some areas of which only ruins remain, before descending back down to the city.

On the way to the centre, I passed through the Albaicín district, which had an oriental flavour.

This impression was reinforced when I reached the cathedral and strolled through the alleyways lined with small oriental shops.

*El Partal*

Then I visited the cathedral, but after the amazing buildings in the other cities, I was no longer impressed. It would certainly have been different if I had done the tour the other way round.

Not far from the cathedral I was lucky again and found a nice Spanish restaurant where I had salad and lasagne. I also had a delicious Rioja from Granada.

A young woman came into the restaurant with an older man who appeared to be her grandfather. She looked sexy and educated at the same time. Purple tights and a checkered skirt adorned her slender legs. She also wore a purple t-shirt and glasses with large frames.

She was talking to the man with such devotion and attention that it moved me. I had to watch her all the time, which she noticed and looked at me out of the corner of her eye.

I listened to her Spanish words without thinking about the content. The words sounded like music to my ears, which I savoured like a symphony concert at the opera as I sipped my Rioja with relish.

I wondered what it was that made me so happy. Was it the usual holiday mood, the activity or simply the effort? Perhaps none of the above. Maybe it was the impressions and the way of life of the people in this wonderful country.

# Málaga

The mountains became smaller in the distance and the landscape began to resemble steppe again. I passed fields of olive trees growing like green tufts out of the dry ground.

*On the way to Málaga*

I hadn't even really arrived in the city when I already hated this place ... Actually, I hated my sat nav, which couldn't tell me clearly how to get to the damn hotel, so I missed the road what felt like a hundred times. Eventually I made it, checked in and explored the city.

In comparison to Granada, I had the feeling that more had been invested in Malaga. The city had been spruced up for tourists. The streets and pavements were in good condition and the squares were nicely decorated.

First, I went up to Gibralfaro Castle, which overlooks the city, to get an overview. The climb was easy compared to the previous walks and I soon reached the top of the viewpoint.

*Viewpoint*

From there I could see the whole city, with the bull-ring standing out like a monument among the apartment blocks.

After the descent I passed the Roman Theatre, of which not much was left. It was a nice place to take a break, which I did. I sat down in the sun, which was now much stronger.

The strolling mile in front of the theatre was being resurfaced. The workmen were sturdily built and moved without haste, as if they were aware of the strong sun and wanted to take their time. The ground had been prepared with smooth sand, and one of the workers knelt in front of it, laying stone on stone and fixing them in place with a rubber mallet. Two other workers prepared the stones and talked to each other with sweeping gestures. The worker laying the stones joined in the conversation, occasionally making a comment without looking up from his work.

Then I went into the old town, which I liked. Everything was nicely done up, the pavements were newly paved, the walls were painted. The place gave the impression that money was at home here.

The cathedral in this town was also impressive, it was almost as big as the one in Seville. It was beautiful and, as in the other cathedrals, there were beautiful paintings and statues to see.

In Málaga, all the sights were quite close together, so despite taking a few breaks, I managed to see everything in a couple of hours. I wasn't quite as blown away as in the other places, but I had already had too many wonderful impressions that were hard to top.

As it wasn't too late, I decided to visit the Picasso Museum. I found the exhibits to be as rich in contrast as I have rarely experienced when visiting a museum.

From impressionist paintings to cubism and sketchy drawings consisting of just a few strokes. I would never have guessed there was a master behind them if it hadn't been written on the sign next to them.

*City park*

Finally, I walked to the city park, which runs parallel to the harbour and was beautifully landscaped. I took another break here and enjoyed the peace and quiet for a while before going back to the hotel to rest.

In the late afternoon I made my way to the harbour. I walked along the promenade, the home of the jet set. Expensive yachts had docked, fine people sat in the sun in the bars. They wore glittering luxury watches on their wrists, thick gold chains showing through their wide-open shirts.

I strolled along this feel-good mile and watched the sun set behind the mountains of Málaga.

*Harbour*

After sunset I went back to the centre to look for a restaurant. The streets were overflowing with people. It was the first day the Christmas lights were switched on. People were streaming into the streets to witness the spectacle. Families stood together, eagerly awaiting the moment they seemed to have been longing for. The atmosphere was as festive as New Year's Eve just before midnight.

When the lights finally came on, countless mobile phones were held up in the air to capture the moment.

This time I chose an Italian restaurant as it was the only one that had seats available. I made myself comfortable in the outdoor area overlooking the pedestrian zone and ordered a pizza and a freshly tapped Spanish beer. It was with some embarrassment that I realised that this Italian pizza had tasted pretty damn good.

I watched the people on the street who seemed incredibly happy. Even if it was just Christmas lights that would be up for a few weeks, the ability to be happy about such an event was enviable. Bright-eyed children, happy mothers, satisfied fathers.

I drank my beer with a feeling of satisfaction and watched as people happily spent the evening.

*Evening in the centre*

# Gibraltar

In the morning I decided to go to Gibraltar one more time. It wasn't a difficult decision as I had already seen everything I was interested in in Málaga.

This day also began with beautiful weather. I drove along the empty motorway, relaxed, just like the week before. I wondered whether it was a mistake to go there again, and if I wouldn't regret it if I didn't find the same magic as the first time. But my doubts quickly disappeared when I saw the rock again in the distance.

I chose the same car park as the first time, picked up my backpack and set off. This time I didn't go in the direction of the Serpentine Street, but walked along the Main Street to the end.

Following my instincts, I walked straight ahead and arrived at the viewpoint from where I had the view of Morocco. I looked out over the glittering sea and gratefully took in the panorama.

Then I looked for the Mediterranean way, because this time I wanted to go the other way. I followed a stony path that wound its way up the cliffs and kept looking out at the gentle waves in the strait between Spain and Morocco.

*Mediterranean way*

Then came the first steps, which I climbed without any problems. I walked up at a leisurely pace, focusing on the scenery around me.

The steps now led directly along the rock and I continued to follow them. I took short breaks to catch my breath and then reached the top without any problems. My shirt was completely soaked with sweat, so the light breeze blowing up there felt refreshing.

While walking down the road, I came across a cyclist who had stopped fifty metres from the end, obviously unable to continue. If he had seen that the finish was so close, he would probably have found the effort bearable and carried on.

A jogger gave up about two hundred metres before the target and abandoned the run, exhausted.

I felt sorry for the athletes, they only gave up because they didn't know how close they were to the finish. The uncertainty about what they didn't know made them give up.

*Blick auf Marokko*

This time there were many more tourists and the number of monkeys had increased accordingly. A young couple were standing in front of a young monkey who was obviously trying to play and was climbing up on the man. The man seemed frightened and uncertain, but was very brave and calm. When another monkey looked at me, I ignored it and continued on my way.

Unfortunately, that wasn't all. When I had to cross a narrow staircase, a full-grown monkey was sitting in the middle of it. I waited for a moment, but he didn't move. Then I walked slowly past him. He watched me closely, looking at my leg, which I pushed just a few centimetres past him, but to my great relief he let me pass.

I passed the cable car station without stopping and continued on to the front viewpoint. Then I took a leisurely stroll down the street.

Back on the Main Street I went down to Grand Casemates Square and had a portion of fish and chips.

Happy with myself and the world, I travelled back to Málaga to spend my last evening there.

# Málaga

After a walk along the harbour, I went into the centre and quickly found a nice Spanish restaurant. I ordered some tapas and had a glass of Rioja.

*View of the pier*

The waiter was friendly and in a good mood. He was worldly and even spoke my language quite well.

When I finished my meal, he poured me a liqueur, which was on the house, and we chatted for a while. He was curious, wanted to know where I was from and told me a lot about Andalusia, its history and development. Many people suffered under the Franco dictatorship, but not everyone agrees, which still causes divisions today. When he told me that the death penalty was only abolished in 1978, I was surprised.

Not without pride, he described the economic development and associated prosperity, which is also thanks to tourism.

He gave me a few tips for excursions, but it was too late for that. I made a few notes anyway, as I was sure I would return here.

Then I took my last walk through the Christmas-lit shopping streets. I thought about how I felt a week ago and how I felt now. Satisfied, I realised that the journey had been more than worth it. I felt good and up to all the challenges. The country gave me the feeling that everything always works out in the end, if you just hang in there. And if you get lost, it's no big deal because you always find your way in the end.

# Hotel information

I booked all my hotels through HRS. A good alternative with similar prices is Booking.com. The prices are from the low season.

Marbella
Puerto Azul Aparthotel, 45 €/Night
Simple beach hotel in a good location

Jerez
Nova Centro, 23 €/Night
Functional hotel, garage included free of charge, location is ok. High praise for the friendly staff.

Sevilla
Catalonia Hispalis, 35 €/Night
Solid middle-class hotel, mainly frequented by business travellers. It is quite far from the centre, but the price is very reasonable.

Cordoba

Eurostars Ciudad de Córdoba, 42 €/Night

Best hotel on the trip. Good location, upper middle class.

Granada

Vita San Anton, 28 €/Night

Mid-range hotel with a great view. Location is good, great value for money.

Malaga

Don Curro, 54 €/Night

The most expensive and least comfortable hotel, with very basic rooms. However, the location was excellent.